Lost Chapters of the Book of Daniel and Related Writings

By Daniel

Copyright © 2019 Lamp of Trismegistus. All rights reserved. No part of this publication may be reproduced or transmitted in any form or by any means, electronic or mechanical, including photocopying, recording, or by any information storage and retrieval system, without permission in writing from Lamp of Trismegistus. Reviewers may quote brief passages.

ISBN: 978-1-63118-417-8

Christian Apocrypha Series

Other Books in this Series and Related Titles

The Lives of Adam and Eve by Moses
(978-1-63118-414-7)

The First and Second Gospels of the Infancy of Jesus Christ by Thomas and James (978-1-63118-415-4)

The Book of the Watchers by Enoch
(978-1-63118-416-1)

Symbolism of the Corner Stone, the North East Corner and the Religious & Masonic Symbolism of Stones by Albert G. Mackey, William Harvey and William Wynn Westcott
(978-1-63118-412-3)

Ancient Mysteries and Secret Societies by Manly P. Hall
(978-1-63118-410-9)

The Influence of Pythagoras on Freemasonry, the Golden Verses of Pythagoras and the Life and Philosophy of Pythagoras by Albert G. Mackey and Manly P. Hall (978-1-63118-320-1)

The Philosophy of Masonry in Five Parts by Roscoe Pound
(978-1-63118-004-0)

Rosicrucian and Masonic Origins by Manly P. Hall
(978-1-63118-000-2)

The Story and Legend of Hiram Abiff by William Harvey, Manly P. Hall and Albert G. Mackey
(978-1-63118-411-6)

Four Lesser Known Masonic Essays by Frank C. Higgins
(978-1-63118-003-3)

Audio Versions are also Available on Audible and iTunes

Table of Contents

Introduction...7

Prologue...9

Part I: The Prayer of Azariah...17

Part II: Song of the Three Holy Children...21

Part III: Susanna and the Elders...27

Part IV: The Priests of Bel...35

Part V: Daniel Slays the Dragon...39

Part VI: Daniel in the Lion's Den...41

Part VII: Seventh Vision pt. 1...43

Part VIII: Seventh Vision pt. 2...47

Part IX: Seventh Vision pt. 3...51

Part X: Seventh Vision pt. 4...55

Part XI: Seventh Vision pt. 5...61

Part XII: Fourteenth Vision...63

Introduction

The Apocrypha are a loosely knit series of books, written by early vanguards of Christianity (covering the eras of both the old and new testaments), and which comprise somewhere between about a dozen to several hundred titles, depending on whom you ask and how that person defines "Apocrypha." A small selection of these can still be found included in the Catholic bible, while a majority of the books in question, were abandoned by church officials in the early centuries of Christianity. Many of these apocryphal books were originally considered canon by early followers of Christ, in the first four centuries following his birth. It wasn't until the meeting of the Council of Nicaea in 325, that Emperor Constantine and a group of roughly 300 church bishops, gathered together with the goal of defining, standardizing and unifying an otherwise splintering Christianity, that many of these writings ceased to be included in the newly established canon. Enjoy then, this book as an example, of just one of the many books of the Christian Apocrypha, and be sure to check out other titles in this series.

Prologue

The apocryphal parts of the Book of Daniel are quite diverse and can be divided into several distinct parts, with the final part being much less commonly encountered. The first six sections of this collection are included in the Roman Catholic bible, but are absent from the modern Protestant bibles. Article 6 of the Thirty-Nine Articles of the Church of England, which contains a list of biblical books that are read "for example of life and instruction of manners", but not for the formation of doctrine, has the first six parts of this collection specifically listed as non-canonical. The remaining five parts of this collection are collectively called *The Seventh Vision of Daniel*.

These first six sections all date to approximately the second century B.C. and were included in the original Greek Septuagint (while the oldest copies of *The Book of Daniel* are entirely in Hebrew and Aramaic). *The Seventh Vision of Daniel*, on the other hand, is likely not as old and may date several hundred years later.

Regarding the Prayer of Azariah and the Song of the Three Holy Children, the origins of these writings are obscure. Whether the accounts were originally composed in Hebrew, Aramaic or Greek is uncertain, although many modern scholars conclude on the basis of textual evidence that there was probably an original Semitic edition.

Regarding Susanna and the Elders, the text itself dates to the second century B.C. and only survives in two separate Greek versions. The passages are believed by most scholars to have never existed in Hebrew or Aramaic, and there are no known early Jewish references to the Susanna story.

Regarding Bel and the Dragon, again, the texts have survived only in Greek. The standard text comes to us from Theodotion, a 2nd-century A.D. revisionist; however, the story of Bel and the Dragon is likely the retelling of a Babylonian fable dating to around 1750 B.C., about an ancient Mesopotamian deity named Marduk, often referred to as "Bel", an ancient Akkadian word meaning "lord."

In regards to the provenance of *The Seventh Vision of Daniel*, two manuscripts containing the text are preserved in the Armenian Library of St. Lazarus, and both copies are paired with a similar but unrelated text entitled *The Vision of Enoch the Righteous*. Jacques Issaverdens, the translator of this current version, notes that *The Seventh Vision of Daniel* was actually included in a copy of the Bible from 1341, which is housed in the aforementioned library. The text of the Seventh Vision was inserted immediately following Daniel's sixth vision, within *The Book of Daniel*. Issaverdens further has this to say, regarding these two texts:

> "The *first of these two Apocrypha, i.e. the Vision of Enoch, is a piece akin to the second, i.e., to Daniel's Seventh Vision; and the subject of both is an allegory which concerns the Byzantine Empire and its historical and religious revolutions and*

vicissitudes. Therefore it is supposed that the author of both must have been a Greek, and consequently the original text from which the Armenian version was made, must have been written in the Greek language.

"As to the antiquity of the original texts, it seems that their date cannot go back to the first centuries; however one may suppose in the beginning, the existence of an ancient and short text, which in later centuries successively received many additions by different people.

"As regards the age of the Armenian version, it is supposed to have been made at the end of the seventh or during the eighth century."

The Prayer of Azariah and the Song of the Three Holy Children is a lengthy passage, consisting of 68 verses, that appears after *Daniel 3:23* in Roman Catholic and Eastern Orthodox Bibles. Following these verses, the Roman Catholic Bible picks up again at *Daniel 3:91*, with what would usually be *Daniel 3:24*.

These 68 verses include three main components. The first is The Prayer of Azariah. The prayer of Daniel's friend Azariah is given while three children were thrown into a fiery furnace for refusing to worship an idol. The second component is a brief account of a radiant figure that met them in the furnace yet was unburned. This is said to be an angel, or interpreted by Christians as a prefigurement or theophany of Jesus Christ, in the same vein as Melchisedek. The third component is The Song of the Three Holy Children, in which the unburned children sing praises once they realize their deliverance.

The Song of the Three Holy Children is part of a hymn sung during the Matins and other services in Orthodoxy. It can be found in the Church of England's *Book of Common Prayer* as the canticle called the "Benedicite" and is one of the traditional canticles that can follow the first scripture lesson in the Order of Morning Prayer.

The story of Susanna and the Elders is 64 verses in length and is included in the extended Book of Daniel as chapter 13, whereas Daniel usually ends at 12 chapters in length.

As the story goes, two lustful elders make false accusations against a Hebrew wife named Susanna, after spying on her, as she bathed in her garden. When she makes her way back to her house, they accost her and threaten to claim that she was meeting a young man in the garden, unless she agrees to have sex with them.

She refuses to be blackmailed and is arrested and about to be put to death for promiscuity when a young man named Daniel interrupts the proceedings, shouting that the elders should be questioned to prevent the death of an innocent woman. After being separated, the two men are cross-examined on the details of what they saw but their testimonies are conflicting, regarding under which tree Susanna supposedly met her lover. In the Greek text, the types of trees cited by the two elders are significant. The first elder says that they were standing under a mastic tree, and Daniel reports that an angel stood ready to *cut* the elder in two. The second elder says that they were standing under an evergreen oak tree, and Daniel reports that an angel stood ready to *saw* the elder in two. The great difference in size between a mastic and an oak makes the elders' lie plain to all the observers. The false accusers are put to death, and virtue triumphs.

The story is notable, as it has inspired numerous artists, writers and musicians over the centuries, to relate the tale in their work, with depictions of the story dating as far back as the 9th century. Painters as diverse as Rembrandt and Picasso have depicted her plight with the elders. Writers as diverse and Shakespeare and Wallace Stevens have referenced the story, and a twentieth century opera on the subject was composed by Carlisle Floyd, in the 1950's.

The story of Bel and the Dragon is 42 verses, broken into three separate narratives, and is included in the extended Book of Daniel by the Roman Catholic and Eastern Orthodox churches as chapter 14, whereas, as stated before, Daniel usually ends at 12 chapters in length.

The first of these narratives is that of The Priests of Bel and is a cautionary tale against the worship of false idols. In it, the king is angered by Daniel's assertion that Bel is an idol made of clay and bronze, rather than a living god who eats and drinks.

To prove otherwise, the king and the priests leave the usual offerings (which were "*twelve great measures of fine flour, and forty sheep, and six vessels of wine*") and then seal the entrance to the temple. The king announces that if Bel does not consume the offerings, the priests are to be sentenced to death; otherwise, Daniel is to be killed.

Daniel then uncovers the ruse, by scattering ashes over the floor of the temple in the presence of the king after the priests have left, and shows that the "sacred" meal of Bel is actually consumed at night by the priests and their wives and children, who enter through a secret door when the temple's doors are sealed.

The next morning, Daniel calls attention to the footprints on the temple floor; the priests of Bel are then arrested and, confessing their deed, reveal the secret passage that they used to sneak inside the temple. They, their wives and children are put to death, and Daniel is permitted to destroy the idol of Bel and the temple. This version has been cited as an ancestor to the traditional "locked room mystery." In addition, it has sometimes been referred to as the world's first detective story.

The second section of the narrative is Daniel Slays the Dragon. In this case the supposed god is no idol, but a living creature, and the same king instructs Daniel to worship it. Instead, Daniel slays the dragon by baking pitch, fat, and hair into cakes that cause the dragon to burst open upon consumption. In other variants, different ingredients serve the purpose, such as straw, nails and hot coals. As a result of killing their idol, the Babylonians demand that Daniel be handed over to them.

The third part of the narrative, Daniel in the Lion's Den, may be a retelling of Daniel's first trip to the lion's den, from *Daniel 6:1-28* or may describe a separate incident. In this version, the story of the lion's den has been made into a consequence of the preceding episode with the dragon. Daniel remains unharmed for a week, in the den with seven lions, and upon seeing this, the king vows to worship the God of Daniel and condemns his detractors to death.

The Seventh Vision of Daniel is aptly named, and normally would follow the six visions mentioned in the canonical *Book of Daniel*. It is part of a tradition referred to as Apocalyptic Literature. The Greek word apocalypse means "revelation" and the numerous works of biblical literature in this category usually involve prophecies or visions of the end-times, as revealed by an angel or other heavenly messenger, often told in heavily veiled and colorful symbolism. Other examples of apocalyptic literature can be found in the earlier chapters of *The Book of Daniel*. Broken into five chapters, the text of *The Seventh Vision of Daniel* begins three years after Gabriel originally appeared to Daniel. In it, the archangel returns to Daniel with visions of the end-times and the Antichrist and warnings of famine and destruction for all, unless mankind changes its ways.

The final piece in this collection is referred to as the *Fourteenth Vision of Daniel*; however, almost nothing is known about it. It was given that title, simply because in the first manuscript of it that was ever found, the text was added immediately following the end of a version of the *Book of Daniel* which had been divided into thirteen parts. While the specific authorship is unknown, scholars believe that it dates to the time of the Third Crusade, thus around 1187.

PART I

The Book of Daniel

Chapter 3, verses 24-45:

The Prayer of Azariah

And they walked in the midst of the fire, praising God, and blessing the Lord.

Then Azariah stood up, and prayed on this manner; and opening his mouth in the midst of the fire said,

Blessed art thou, O Lord God of our fathers: thy name is worthy to be praised and glorified for evermore:

For thou art righteous in all the things that thou hast done to us: yea, true are all thy works, thy ways are right, and all thy judgments truth.

In all the things that thou hast brought upon us, and upon the holy city of our fathers, even Jerusalem, thou hast executed true judgment: for according to truth and judgment didst thou bring all these things upon us because of our sins.

For we have sinned and committed iniquity, departing from

thee.

In all things have we trespassed, and not obeyed thy commandments, nor kept them, neither done as thou hast commanded us, that it might go well with us.

Wherefore all that thou hast brought upon us, and every thing that thou hast done to us, thou hast done in true judgment.

And thou didst deliver us into the hands of lawless enemies, most hateful forsakers of God, and to an unjust king, and the most wicked in all the world.

And now we cannot open our mouths, we are become a shame and reproach to thy servants; and to them that worship thee.

Yet deliver us not up wholly, for thy name's sake, neither disannul thou thy covenant:

And cause not thy mercy to depart from us, for thy beloved Abraham's sake, for thy servant Issac's sake, and for thy holy Israel's sake;

To whom thou hast spoken and promised, that thou wouldest multiply their seed as the stars of heaven, and as the sand that lieth upon the seashore.

For we, O Lord, are become less than any nation, and be kept under this day in all the world because of our sins.

Neither is there at this time prince, or prophet, or leader, or burnt offering, or sacrifice, or oblation, or incense, or place to sacrifice before thee, and to find mercy.

Nevertheless in a contrite heart and an humble spirit let us be accepted.

Like as in the burnt offerings of rams and bullocks, and like as in ten thousands of fat lambs: so let our sacrifice be in thy sight this day, and grant that we may wholly go after thee: for they shall not be confounded that put their trust in thee.

And now we follow thee with all our heart, we fear thee, and seek thy face.

Put us not to shame: but deal with us after thy loving kindness, and according to the multitude of thy mercies.

Deliver us also according to thy marvelous works, and give glory to thy name, O Lord: and let all them that do thy servants hurt be ashamed;

And let them be confounded in all their power and might, and let their strength be broken;

And let them know that thou art God, the only God, and glorious over the whole world.

PART II

The Book of Daniel

Chapter 3, verses 46-90:

Song of the Three Holy Children

And the king's servants, that put them in, ceased not to make the oven hot with rosin, pitch, tow, and small wood;

So that the flame streamed forth above the furnace forty and nine cubits.

And it passed through, and burned those Chaldeans it found about the furnace.

But the angel of the Lord came down into the oven together with Azariah and his fellows, and smote the flame of the fire out of the oven;

And made the midst of the furnace as it had been a moist whistling wind, so that the fire touched them not at all, neither hurt nor troubled them.

Then the three, as out of one mouth, praised, glorified, and blessed, God in the furnace, saying,

Blessed art thou, O Lord God of our fathers: and to be praised and exalted above all forever.

And blessed is thy glorious and holy name: and to be praised and exalted above all forever.

Blessed art thou in the temple of thine holy glory: and to be praised and glorified above all forever.

Blessed art thou that beholdest the depths, and sittest upon the cherubims: and to be praised and exalted above all forever.

Blessed art thou on the glorious throne of thy kingdom: and to be praised and glorified above all forever.

Blessed art thou in the firmament of heaven: and above all to be praised and glorified forever.

O all ye works of the Lord, bless ye the Lord: praise and exalt him above all forever,

O ye heavens, bless ye the Lord: praise and exalt him above all forever.

O ye angels of the Lord, bless ye the Lord: praise and exalt him above all forever.

O all ye waters that be above the heaven, bless ye the Lord: praise and exalt him above all forever.

O all ye powers of the Lord, bless ye the Lord: praise and

exalt him above all forever.

O ye sun and moon, bless ye the Lord: praise and exalt him above all forever.

O ye stars of heaven, bless ye the Lord: praise and exalt him above all for ver.

O every shower and dew, bless ye the Lord: praise and exalt him above all forever.

O all ye winds, bless ye the Lord: praise and exalt him above all forever,

O ye fire and heat, bless ye the Lord: praise and exalt him above all forever.

O ye winter and summer, bless ye the Lord: praise and exalt him above all forever.

O ye dews and storms of snow, bless ye the Lord: praise and exalt him above all forever.

O ye nights and days, bless ye the Lord: bless and exalt him above all forever.

O ye light and darkness, bless ye the Lord: praise and exalt him above all forever.

O ye ice and cold, bless ye the Lord: praise and exalt him above all forever.

O ye frost and snow, bless ye the Lord: praise and exalt him above all forever.

O ye lightnings and clouds, bless ye the Lord: praise and exalt him above all forever.

O let the earth bless the Lord: praise and exalt him above all forever.

O ye mountains and little hills, bless ye the Lord: praise and exalt him above all forever.

O all ye things that grow in the earth, bless ye the Lord: praise and exalt him above all forever.

O ye mountains, bless ye the Lord: Praise and exalt him above all forever.

O ye seas and rivers, bless ye the Lord: praise and exalt him above all forever.

O ye whales, and all that move in the waters, bless ye the Lord: praise and exalt him above all forever.

O all ye fowls of the air, bless ye the Lord: praise and exalt him above all forever.

O all ye beasts and cattle, bless ye the Lord: praise and exalt him above all forever.

O ye children of men, bless ye the Lord: praise and exalt

him above all forever.

O Israel, bless ye the Lord: praise and exalt him above all forever.

O ye priests of the Lord, bless ye the Lord: praise and exalt him above all forever.

O ye servants of the Lord, bless ye the Lord: praise and exalt him above all forever.

O ye spirits and souls of the righteous, bless ye the Lord: praise and exalt him above all forever.

O ye holy and humble men of heart, bless ye the Lord: praise and exalt him above all forever.

O Ananias, Azariah, and Misael, bless ye the Lord: praise and exalt him above all for ever: far he hath delivered us from hell, and saved us from the hand of death, and delivered us out of the midst of the furnace and burning flame: even out of the midst of the fire hath he delivered us.

O give thanks unto the Lord, because he is gracious: for his mercy endureth forever.

O all ye that worship the Lord, bless the God of gods, praise him, and give him thanks: for his mercy endureth forever.

PART III

The Book of Daniel

Chapter 13, verses 1-64:

Susanna and the Elders

There dwelt a man in Babylon, called Joacim:

And he took a wife, whose name was Susanna, the daughter of Chelcias, a very fair woman, and one that feared the Lord.

Her parents also were righteous, and taught their daughter according to the Law of Moses.

Now Joacim was a great rich man, and had a fair garden joining unto his house: and to him resorted the Jews; because he was more honorable than all others.

The same year were appointed two of the ancients of the people to be judges, such as the Lord spoke of, that wickedness came from Babylon from ancient judges, who seemed to govern the people.

These kept much at Joacim's house: and all that had any suits in law came unto them.

Now when the people departed away at noon, Susanna went into her husband's garden to walk.

And the two elders saw her going in every day, and walking; so that their lust was inflamed toward her.

And they perverted their own mind, and turned away their eyes, that they might not look unto heaven, nor remember just judgments.

And albeit they both were wounded with her love, yet darest not one show the other his grief.

For they were ashamed to declare their lust, that they desired to have to do with her.

Yet they watched diligently from day to day to see her.

And the one said to the other, Let us now go home: for it is dinner time.

So when they were gone out, they parted the one from the other, and turning back again they came to the same place; and after that they had asked one another the cause, they acknowledged their lust: then appointed they a time both together, when they might find her alone.

And it fell out, as they watched a fit time, she went in as before with two maids only, and she was desirous to wash herself in the garden: for it was hot.

And there was no body there save the two elders, that had hid themselves, and watched her.

Then she said to her maids, Bring me oil and washing balls, and shut the garden doors, that I may wash me.

And they did as she bade them, and shut the garden doors, and went out themselves at privy doors to fetch the things that she had commanded them: but they saw not the elders, because they were hid.

Now when the maids were gone forth, the two elders rose up, and ran unto her, saying,

Behold, the garden doors are shut, that no man can see us, and we are in love with thee; therefore consent unto us, and lie with us.

If thou wilt not, we will bear witness against thee, that a young man was with thee: and therefore thou didst send away thy maids from thee.

Then Susanna sighed, and said, I am straitened on every side: for if I do this thing, it is death unto me: and if I do it not I cannot escape your hands.

It is better for me to fall into your hands, and not do it, than to sin in the sight of the Lord.

With that Susanna cried with a loud voice: and the two elders cried out against her.

Then ran the one, and opened the garden door.

So when the servants of the house heard the cry in the garden, they rushed in at the privy door, to see what was done unto her.

But when the elders had declared their matter, the servants were greatly ashamed: for there was never such a report made of Susanna.

And it came to pass the next day, when the people were assembled to her husband Joacim, the two elders came also full of mischievous imagination against Susanna to put her to death;

And said before the people, Send for Susanna, the daughter of Chelcias, Joacim's wife. And so they sent.

So she came with her father and mother, her children, and all her kindred.

Now Susanna was a very delicate woman, and beauteous to behold.

And these wicked men commanded to uncover her face, (for she was covered) that they might be filled with her beauty.

Therefore her friends and all that saw her wept.

Then the two elders stood up in the midst of the people, and laid their hands upon her head.

And she weeping looked up toward heaven: for her heart trusted in the Lord.

And the elders said, As we walked in the garden alone, this woman came in with two maids, and shut the garden doors, and sent the maids away.

Then a young man, who there was hid, came unto her, and lay with her.

Then we that stood in a corner of the garden, seeing this wickedness, ran unto them.

And when we saw them together, the man we could not hold: for he was stronger than we, and opened the door, and leaped out.

But having taken this woman, we asked who the young man was, but she would not tell us: these things do we testify.

Then the assembly believed them as those that were the elders and judges of the people: so they condemned her to death.

Then Susanna cried out with a loud voice, and said, O everlasting God, that knowest the secrets, and knowest all things before they be:

Thou knowest that they have borne false witness against me, and, behold, I must die; whereas I never did such things as these men have maliciously invented against me.

And the Lord heard her voice.

Therefore when she was led to be put to death, the Lord raised up the holy spirit of a young youth whose name was Daniel:

Who cried with a loud voice, I am clear from the blood of this woman.

Then all the people turned them toward him, and said, What mean these words that thou hast spoken?

So he standing in the midst of them said, Are ye such fools, ye sons of Israel, that without examination or knowledge of the truth ye have condemned a daughter of Israel?

Return again to the place of judgment: for they have borne false witness against her.

Wherefore all the people turned again in haste, and the elders said unto him, Come, sit down among us, and show it us, seeing God hath given thee the honor of an elder.

Then said Daniel unto them, Put these two aside one far from another, and I will examine them.

So when they were put asunder one from another, he called one of them, and said unto him, O thou that art waxen old in wickedness, now thy sins which thou hast committed aforetime are come to light.

For thou hast pronounced false judgment and hast condemned the innocent and hast let the guilty go free; albeit the Lord saith, The innocent and righteous shalt thou not slay.

Now then, if thou hast seen her, tell me, Under what tree sawest thou them companying together? Who answered, Under a mastick tree.

And Daniel said, Very well; thou hast lied against thine own head; for even now the angel of God hath received the sentence of God to cut thee in two.

So he put him aside, and commanded to bring the other, and said unto him, O thou seed of Chanaan, and not of Juda, beauty hath deceived thee, and lust hath perverted thine heart.

Thus have ye dealt with the daughters of Israel, and they for fear companied with you: but the daughter of Juda would not abide your wickedness.

Now therefore tell me, Under what tree didst thou take them companying together? Who answered, Under an holm tree.

Then said Daniel unto him, Well; thou hast also lied against thine own head: for the angel of God waiteth with the sword to saw thee in two, that he may destroy you.

With that all the assembly cried out with a loud voice, and praised God, who saveth them that trust in him.

And they arose against the two elders, for Daniel had convicted them of false witness by their own mouth:

And according to the Law of Moses they did unto them in such sort as they maliciously intended to do to their neighbor: and they put them to death. Thus the innocent blood was saved the same day.

Therefore Chelcias and his wife praised God for their daughter Susanna, with Joacim her husband, and all the kindred, because there was no dishonesty found in her.

From that day forth was Daniel had in great reputation in the sight of the people.

Part IV

The Book of Daniel

Chapter 14, verses 1-22:

The Priests of Bel

And king Astyages was gathered to his fathers, and Cyrus of Persia received his kingdom.

And Daniel conversed with the king, and was honored above all his friends.

Now the Babylons had an idol, called Bel, and there were spent upon him every day twelve great measures of fine flour, and forty sheep, and six vessels of wine.

And the king worshipped it and went daily to adore it: but Daniel worshipped his own God. And the king said unto him, Why dost not thou worship Bel?

Who answered and said, Because I may not worship idols made with hands, but the living God, who hath created the heaven and the earth, and hath sovereignty over all flesh.

Then said the king unto him, Thinkest thou not that Bel is

a living God? seest thou not how much he eateth and drinketh every day?

Then Daniel smiled, and said, O king, be not deceived: for this is but clay within, and brass without, and did never eat or drink any thing.

So the king was wroth, and called for his priests, and said unto them, If ye tell me not who this is that devoureth these expenses, ye shall die.

But if ye can certify me that Bel devoureth them, then Daniel shall die: for he hath spoken blasphemy against Bel. And Daniel said unto the king, Let it be according to thy word.

Now the priests of Bel were threescore and ten, beside their wives and children. And the king went with Daniel into the temple of Bel.

So Bel's priests said, Lo, we go out: but thou, O king, set on the meat, and make ready the wine, and shut the door fast and seal it with thine own signet;

And tomorrow when thou comest in, if thou findest not that hath eaten up all, we will suffer death, or else Daniel, that speaketh falsely against us.

And they little regarded it: for under the table they had made a privy entrance, whereby they entered in continually, and consumed those things.

So when they were gone forth, the king set meats before Bel. Now Daniel had commanded his servants to bring ashes, and those they strewed throughout all the temple in the presence of the king alone: then went they out, and shut the door, and sealed it with the king's signet, and so departed.

Now in the night came the priests with their wives and children, as they were wont to do, and did eat and drink up all.

In the morning betime the king arose, and Daniel with him.

And the king said, Daniel, are the seals whole? And he said, Yea, O king, they be whole.

And as soon as he had opened the door, the king looked upon the table, and cried with a loud voice, Great art thou, O Bel, and with thee is no deceit at all.

Then laughed Daniel, and held the king that he should not go in, and said, Behold now the pavement, and mark well whose footsteps are these.

And the king said, I see the footsteps of men, women, and children. And then the king was angry,

And took the priests with their wives and children, who showed him the privy doors, where they came in, and consumed such things as were upon the table.

Therefore the king slew them, and delivered Bel into Daniel's power, who destroyed him and his temple.

38

Part V

The Book of Daniel

Chapter 14, verses 23-30:

Daniel Slays the Dragon

And in that same place there was a great dragon, which they of Babylon worshipped.

And the king said unto Daniel, Wilt thou also say that this is of brass? lo, he liveth, he eateth and drinketh; thou canst not say that he is no living god: therefore worship him.

Then said Daniel unto the king, I will worship the Lord my God: for he is the living God.

But give me leave, O king, and I shall slay this dragon without sword or staff. The king said, I give thee leave.

Then Daniel took pitch, and fat, and hair, and did seethe them together, and made lumps thereof: this he put in the dragon's mouth, and so the dragon burst in sunder: and Daniel said, Lo, these are the gods ye worship.

When they of Babylon heard that, they took great

indignation, and conspired against the king, saying, The king is become a Jew, and he hath destroyed Bel, he hath slain the dragon, and put the priests to death.

So they came to the king, and said, Deliver us Daniel, or else we will destroy thee and thine house.

Now when the king saw that they pressed him sore, being constrained, he delivered Daniel unto them:

Part VI

The Book of Daniel

Chapter 14, verses 31-42:

Daniel in the Lion's Den

Who cast him into the lions' den: where he was six days.

And in the den there were seven lions, and they had given them every day two carcasses, and two sheep: which then were not given to them, to the intent they might devour Daniel.

Now there was in Jewry a prophet, called Habakkuk, who had made pottage, and had broken bread in a bowl, and was going into the field, for to bring it to the reapers.

But the angel of the Lord said unto Habakkuk: Go, carry the dinner that thou hast into Babylon unto Daniel, who is in the lions' den.

And Habakkuk said, Lord, I never saw Babylon; neither do I know where the den is.

Then the angel of the Lord took him by the crown, and bare him by the hair of his head, and through the vehemency of his spirit set him in Babylon over the den.

And Habakkuk cried, saying, O Daniel, Daniel, take the dinner which God hath sent thee.

And Daniel said, Thou hast remembered me, O God, neither hast thou forsaken them that seek thee and love thee.

So Daniel arose, and did eat; and the angel of the Lord set Habakkuk in his own place again immediately.

Upon the seventh day the king went to bewail Daniel, and when he came to the den, he looked in, and behold, Daniel was sitting.

Then cried the king with a loud voice, saying: Great art Lord God of Daniel, and there is none other beside thee.

And he drew him out, and cast those that were the cause of his destruction into the den, and they were devoured in a moment before his face.

Part VII

The Seventh Vision of Daniel

Chapter One

Three years after all the revelations that had been made to Daniel the prophet, the angel Gabriel, who had aforetime been sent unto him, was sent again by the Lord and said unto him: Daniel, beloved man, I am sent by the Lord to speak to thee, and to shew thee what shall happen at the end of the days, after the coming of the Word, who shall be announced by me.

There shall be a virgin in Israel and she shall receive the Word from the Word, and He will take flesh for the sake of the world, and will cause many among Israel to be saved. And consider with care, and hear what shall happen at the end of the days in all the towns and provinces, on account of the iniquities of men.

And I, Daniel, said: Speak on, my Lord.

And he spake unto me, saying: After the fulfillment of all that was prophesied concerning all the towns and provinces of Asia, Pontus, Phrygia, Galatia, Cappadocia, Carpatia, Smyrna, Antioch, Alexandria, Egypt, Nicaea, Nicomedia, Calcedon, Byzantium, Babylon and Rome, through the mourning of the children and the increase of the dearth, the fertile land shall be laid waste; thy princes shall become children of groanings, and thy possessions that are around thee shall be made desolate, and they shall be removed from thee to Babylon of the Seven-Hills. The prince of Pontus shall fall, and the sword shall devour his children; his hosts shall fall by the edge of the sword, and many shall be carried over to Byzantium and there they shall be buried.

The children of the Phrygians shall be consumed through the want of bread and water; their land shall be cleft and they shall be meat unto all the fowls of the air, and many of them shall flee to Carthage.

In Galatia a fire from heaven shall appear, and she shall be consumed by thunders and lightnings. The thrones of her princes shall be overthrown, and her south country shall be bathed in blood and burnt with fire; and then many shall flee to Rome.

In Cappadocia Minor, her children shall destroy one another, and carry one another captive, and their princes shall be discomfited; and all they who dwell around her shall be in tribulation and shall sigh heavily.

The children of Babylon Minor and Carpatia, shall be in tribulation, they shall see conflagrations and they shall not believe; the ground shall be cleft and they shall all be brought down to hell, and many shall flee to the Seven-Hills.

In Smyrna wrath shall be increased; she, like a cup, shall be filled up with blood, and she shall fall down from her glory. Thy princes shall be carried away, and thy great ones shall be overthrown; for the day of the Lord's wrath shall come upon thee.

The children of Antioch shall perish, and her buildings shall be thrown down, and her princes shall not enjoy them. Thy fall shall be wrought by an earthquake, and thy great wealth shall cause thee to perish.

In Alexandria many tumults of war shall take place, — and the neck of her impertinence until the trenches of her ramparts — her princes shall be driven away.

The children of the Egyptians, harassed by famine, shall flee away. Thy possessions shall be reduced to nothing, the Nile shall be drained and thy princes shall perish.

The daughters of the Nicaeans shall be in mourning and in sorrow on account of their kinsmen and their husbands who shall be made captive by warriors; and thy princes shall become servants to those whom they know not.

Woe unto thee Nicomedia, who hast lifted up thine horn and hast devoured the bodies of thy saints that were in thee; thou shall perish through the blood of righteous men, who shall give thee like for like, and thou shalt be cast down to hell. Mourn and lament, thou wretched one! for thou shall be utterly destroyed with thy children. Thy princes are princes of sighs, and thy priests fond of gold and silver, and the beauty of thy splendor, shall fade.

O Carthage and thou people of the Persians! what shall happen to thee at the end of the days, thou knowest not; and at the end of all ages how long shall thine existence last after that of all the towns and provinces? Thou, city decked with gold and silver, and ye, people adorned and embellished, shall perish by famine. There shall be great rioting in thee, and thy children shall amuse themselves with gold and then they shall be consumed by dearth. The land of Byzantium and that of Babylon shall sink, warriors shall seize it, its foundations shall be destroyed and its strength shall be crushed.

Rome shall have no prince at that time, but her arms shall be sharpened, her arrows hardened, and her perfidy increased. Many times shall a prince rise up in her, and again shall he fall, and she shall be reduced to three streets. Many shall fear thee, O Rome, on account of the splendor of thy numerous princes, and on account of thine haughty arrogance and thy great wealth.

Part VIII

The Seventh Vision of Daniel

Chapter Two

The children of Byzantium shall work wonders; for a man of Byzant shall, depart from her and shall go into the so-called Seven-Hills, and shall strengthen her foundations; her name shall be spread throughout all the inhabitants of the world, and throughout all the different tongues. And again a wonderful man, born of a remarkable woman, shall rebuild her. And in due time the wish of his heart shall be fulfilled, for he shall find the Wood of Life, and his scepter shall become great. He shall find nails that were on the same sign, and he shall put them on his bridles for the sake of salvation and of victory in battle. His horn shall be exalted and mighty, and his name shall be acclaimed in all tongues, and an everlasting remembrance shall be granted to that city.

And after him shall arise the second scepter, that shall shed the blood of righteous men. He shall proclaim the commandments, but he shall not acknowledge God, and with a blind heart he shall touch the Holy Scriptures. And after him one that is a philosopher, shall come to thee, Babylon of the Seven-Hills, and he shall erect in thee an idol, but for that thou shalt not suffer violence.

And after all this there shall arise exalted horns and very great scepters, and they shall prevail against thee, and they shall be held in great remembrance. And another greater scepter shall prevail exceedingly, and shall be exalted for the sake of the Lord's name; for God's gift is in him. Through him life shall be glorious, and through his cheerfulness all men shall rejoice and and from the towns and provinces people shall gather in thee, and shall come unto thee, the Seven Hills; and each one shall work at his own work, and the scepter of the kingdom shall prevail until the end of its days.

And from one scepter shall come forth two scepters; and one of thy scepters shall become a wild beast, and the second of thy scepters an animal, in the two streets of the Seven-Hills. From Rome there shall come unto thee great glory like a cup filled up, until thy time shall arrive. First, the city shall be full of singing, and secondly, thy wealth as a gushing fountain, shall be for all. Thou shalt be decked like a bride, and yet thou shalt appear like a widow. Thy bunches of grapes, abundantly fruitful as they were, shall diminish, and thy great glory shall be divided and the kingdom that is in thee shall fall.

And another scepter shall arise called Theodosius, and he shall walk in holiness, and his name shall be consecrated in thee, the Seven-Hills! And thy children shall rejoice in his birth, and each one shall do as he listeth. All the towns and provinces shall serve thee, and thine abundance shall be a source of great prosperity to all the world. And the Nile of the Egyptians shall give thee to drink, and thou shalt become a bulwark of the Church, and there shall be great fear and trembling before thy scepter; and this is the beginning of sighs of thy kingdom. And the time of his scepter shall be long and very wonderful; and his scepter shall conquer unto the extremities of the earth, from the east and the west and from the north and the south. And his neck shall be firm, and his right hand strong, and his years many more than the years of any other king. And after all this he shall turn his face towards his father, and the number of his years shall be great; and his name shall be terrible, and his kingdom full of splendor.

And another, a third king, shall be in Rome, O thou Seven-Hills! Thou hast been called Seven-Hills, because all the peoples of the Persians shall come unto thee, and thou, Rome, shalt never again reign to the end of all the ages. Thy second king shall reign in old age, and his name is Marcianus, and the duration of his reign shall be shorter than the reign of the first; and his kingdom shall be far more formidable. And that time shall be to some for good and to others for evil. And his kingdom shall be for times, and for hours, and for half an hour. Thy builder, O thou Seven-Hills I shall make a present of thee unto him, and he shall raise thee up unto him through the Book of the Faith, and a great rupture shall take place in his kingdom. The priests shall fall from their places, many towns shall be overthrown, and many conversions shall take place amongst men, and thy beauty, O thou Seven-Hills! and thine extent shall not diminish. And after all this, even he shall die with his fathers, and the other scepter shall reign in thee and he shall be a wild beast, and he shall receive the first scepter which shall at length be beaten by the dog. And this wild beast shall be, like the first scepter, great and strong in words and in wisdom; and he shall not be despised by his nobles; and his neck shall be like the neck of a bullock, and his eyes like the eyes of a lion; he shall roar fearfully, and all towns and provinces shall tremble before his horns. And during his time the rainbow shall appear in heaven, and there shall be all kinds of signs in heaven, and upon the earth shall be heard the noise of thunders and the falling of many towns. The earth shall be cloven asunder, buildings shall be overthrown from their foundations, and her paths shall be of fire. And there shall be fightings in it and in thee, the Seven-Hills; and thy gorgeous buildings shall be burnt with fire, and thy glory shall be razed to the ground, and thy children shall moan in thee, and thy great joy shall turn into mourning, and thy children shall drag along the ground the bodies of thy great ones. Suddenly a storm shall come down from heaven and shall cover the earth, and dragon-like peoples shall appear on earth, and many shall grow poor, and many indigent people shall grow rich, and a great riot shall take place in thee. Ye warriors in Thrace and in Cilicia! shout with arms and swords!

Part IX

The Seventh Vision of Daniel

Chapter Three

And at that time the wild beast shall send his sword to the east, and shall not be able to prevail; and a man who is shaped like a dragon from the loins upward, shall despise him; and with this man be shall send his second sword to the west, and he shall not be able to conquer him, and the dragon shall be despised by the dog. The wild beast shall be oppressed by the dog through many presents and much gold and riches. And the dog shall rise up against the wild beast, and shall make his whelps rise against the throne of the wild beast and against the scepters; and the dog shall cause the wild beast to perish and his dens to be captured. And the dogs shall drive out the wild beast, and all men shall perceive that the dog persecutes the lion. And the lion shall return and shall slay the dog and his whelps. And the lion shall roar with a very great roaring, and his roaring shall be heard throughout all the towns and provinces, and his dens shall inspire terror. And men shall be disconcerted amongst themselves on account of the roaring of the lion, and of the death of the dog.

And the second dog, by transforming his tongue, shall drive back the lion to his den, and shall depart from him when he shall no longer be able to resist him. And the dog's whelp shall conceal himself for times, and for a time, and for an hour, and in his time he shall reign, and his name shall be "Whelp of dog", which being translated means: "King of peoples". And the wild beast shall root out the remembrance of the dog. As they shall have known it previously, they shall spread calumny about him, and they will destroy his image in his town, and many shall meditate slaying him in the wild beast's den, and they shall not resist him. And his colleagues in authority shall die by the sword in another town, and well shall they know the prayers of the priest for the sake of the unknown ones. And one of the great ones, a young man from amongst the warriors of the wild beast, will send to the beast many people bound hand and foot. And then when the wild beast shall make many his servants from amongst the different peoples, and as a lord shall call them to him, another man shall present himself unto him and shall take him in his bosom. And he shall drive away the warrior men, and he himself shall be driven away by them, and shall flee from them on foot, and nobody shall overtake him, for he is swift of foot, and he shall flee to the wild beast and shall enter into his bosom. And the little wild beast shall go out unto him and shall be inspired with courage; and the big wild beast shall make him to sit on his throne, and cause him to be his colleague in authority and on the throne a substitute for himself. And the two wild beasts shall dwell in one cavern; the whelp shall be emboldened to make war, and the wild beast shall return to his own land from whence he came. And the little wild beast shall occupy his place until a certain time, being crowned king by no one, but through his own violence; and he shall come into the snares of the kingdom, and the young wild beast shall return to the big wild beast. And leaving the snares to him who made them, he shall rule over thee, the Seven-Hills, and shall oppress thee. His rejoicing shall be great, he will give himself up to pleasure and be beloved by the great ones, but many shall hate him. He shall grant life and abundance, and the dragon shall play with him, and with the hunting rod of the wild beast shall drag him along.

Woe to thee in that time, thou Seven-Hills, Babylon! when the widow shall reign, and the dragon shall drive away the stranger, and the stranger that is called Salamander shall flee, turning his face toward the islands; — gold and silver and precious stones, and the crowns of the scepters; and he who is in the bosom of the wild beast, tripled by the Persian people of Carthage, — none of the men shall drive him away because of the love of the dragon and of thy great splendor that was in thee. And he shall be driven about from land to land, and shall be oppressed by the strangers. And being oppressed by the strangers in sustenance and by journeys, he shall send up his sighs unto his Creator along with his innocent ones. And the hunting-rod which came forth from the wild beast shall be allied with the dog, and the dragon shall occupy the place of oppression and of trial, — following with his worthless thrones, — and shall make war on the holy place. And the dragon with his tongue shall utter threats against holy men and against the holy relics; and shall suppress the government of the patriarchs, and take by force the holy churches; and they who shall dwell in the holes and the caves and in the clefts of the earth, shall come unto thee, the Seven-Hills, to escape from the tyranny of the dragon.

And after all this they shall shake off the dust from their feet in thee, suffering martyrdom at his hands. Then the beauty of thy magnificence shall be burnt with fire; and a young man shall flee away under pretense of carrying with his hunting-rod the first wild beast, who is called Salamander. Then in that time the dragon shall suffer oppression, and he shall be taken by his successors, and shall be bound by those that are at his left, and nobody shall receive him, because he shed the blood of holy men in the towns and in the provinces. And he shall flee into the holy temple which he previously had usurped, and nobody shall receive him, for plagues from heaven shall be upon him. And the young- man shall come to Salamander, and he shall cause the stranger to advance before the dragon; and the dragon seeing him shall flee away from him, and the stranger shall not slay the dragon; he will keep him away from his presence. And the young man shall fall, and great shall his fall be; and the widow shall not escape; and they shall cause her to see the stranger and his colleague on the throne, and she shall become tributary in the tabernacles of him who created her, and at her throne shall be required the blood of her father. And in a short time the stranger shall become great, and there shall be abundance in thee, Seven-Hills! and many shall die amongst the men who are assembled in thee from the towns and provinces.

Part X

The Seventh Vision of Daniel

Chapter Four

And at that time there shall be earthquakes in divers places, and they shall hear the voice of many people and they will not believe. And thy wealth and thy glory made thee as sad as thou wast proud before; and thine ambition humbled thee; but great abundance and beauty shall be in thee. The end of the time shall come to thee, and from thee shall come forth the hunting-rod that proceeds from the wild beast, and he will go to the dwellings of the strangers. Then thy daughters shall adorn themselves to be a snare to the young men to kill many of them, and thy great ones shall fall, and many tribulations and troubles shall take place.

Then the angel of death shall strike thee with all the towns and provinces, and violent deaths shall be sent down from heaven. Suddenly he shall be excited against the earth; the earth shall shake and the temples shall fall, and the houses shall become graves. And the sea shall make its waves foam up, and shall cover men, and there shall be some who shall flee away and be saved. Then a gathering of angels shall take place, and they shall present themselves in prayer before the throne.

Then shalt thou, Seven-Hills, Babylon! mourn for thy

children, lying in sackcloth and casting ashes on thy head, when thou shalt see men perish on account of their sins and transgressions; both men with children and women with sucking babes shall perish, because the Lord's wrath is upon them. Thy defenses shall be cloven asunder and thy tabernacles shall be razed to the ground; sucking children with parched mouths shall cry unto God, and thy priests shall fret themselves and weep. Thy great ones, thy scepters and thy citizens shall mourn sorely, and thy travelers shall be in pain; thy bunches of grapes shall fall, and thy vineyards shall fail. The earth shall be cleft with a great shock and shall cause men to perish, from the sucking child to the old man. But the Lord shall not cause thee to perish wholly, thou Seven-Hills! for the time of thy destruction is not yet come; the gulf shall open to swallow up men, but it shall not engulf them, for thy time is not yet come. Torments are prepared for thee, for thou hast committed all kinds of iniquity, having received the earth in thy bosom, and men shall be in great anguish until the Lord shall send from heaven to destroy them.

But the counsels of the Lord shall appear from the punishment that must take place, and those who have found refuge in thee shall suffer torments. The people that placed their hope in thee, and the hunting-rod, shall make thee perish. The whelp shall drive away the whelp, requiring the blood of his fathers, and of his own will shall he give himself up to strangers, to the dogs and to their companions. And he shall raise up tongues and peoples and shall rule over many nations; and the two dogs shall fight against one another, and shall destroy each other.

Woe, when the widow shall reign, and shall secretly conspire against the strangers! and the other stranger will seek her ruin and shall perfidiously destroy her. And those days shall be painful and calamitous. The children of the scepters shall be in tumult and shall fight against one another, and then men shall suffer much pain and misery, such as they have never before known. And the prince, the believer, shall not trust in the Salamander, because he is a stranger, and they shall receive from his people what they did not ask. And the Salamander would fain flee away, but he shall not be able, for Placitas shall reach him and shall kill him.

And the other scepter shall rule in thee, O Seven-Hills, and many afflictions shall take place. A poor man shall come up who shall not acknowledge favors; a haughty man, fond of gold, warlike, and his name is Orloghius; and his throne shall last few days, and he shall be swift to anger. And his nobles shall hate him, and his townsmen shall be vexed. Wrath from heaven shall be during his days; many times he shall harass Babylon. During the time of his reign sad news shall arrive for thee, and the troops of barbarians shall alarm thee and they shall not fight.

Then another tyrant king shall come up, and shall fight against him and shall drive him away; and he will slay him with great affliction and groaning. And this king shall reign and shall take hold of the scepter that is in thee, the Seven-Hills! and he shall be the greatest among very great and glorious thrones, and that man shall be valiant on the right hand and on the left. And during his time there shall be a great famine and not a small one, and the earth shall become uninhabited by men; abundant water-courses shall flow out, and the sky shall become gloomy and agitated, thy vineyards shall diminish, thy beauties shall be deformed, the days shall be shortened and one day shall be dwarfed to six hours. Woe, to the men that shall be in that time!

And the king shall turn his face to the west. Then woe to thee, the Seven-Hills, when thy king is a young man. In that time a great peril shall overtake thee; there shall be a man who shall know his brother's wife, and the son his mother, and the daughter shall go up to her father's bed, the brother shall know his sister, and there shall be multiplied blasphemies, murders, oaths, slanders, falsehoods, obscenities, sufferings, abuses of authority, hatred, mutinies, and bloodshed in the temple of the holy ministers. And kings shall arise against kings, princes against princes, the powerful against the poor, and the rich and the poor shall perish. And Bithynia, which is on the sea-shore, shall be destroyed by an earthquake; and the waves of the sea shall mount up and overflow and cover the foundations of Bithynia, as far as the little town of Nicomedia. And again another king shall arise, and his time shall be for a few days only. He shall be wicked and very terrible. And henceforth there shall be no good season, but a bad one; his son shall make war against him and shall destroy him by the sword.

And another king shall arise of another religion, an Arian, and shall draw all to himself. Woe to thee, O Seven-Hills, at that time, for more than all thou shalt mourn for thyself and thy boundaries! After this, kings and princes, and chiefs and champions shall rise against towns and provinces and places, and there shall be riots and confusions amongst men. A barbarous people shall fall upon the towns and the provinces; and, because of the multitude of the people, the earth shall sink seventy-three cubits. And thou, O Seven-Hills, shalt not be vexed by them; but a war of thine own shall afflict thee, and the beauty of the earth shall diminish in thee; wrath from heaven shall be upon thee and a great scourge; and a pillar of fire shall appear stretching from heaven to earth. Then thy kingdom shall be removed and thou shalt remain in eternal pollution, and thus thou shalt he consumed by dearth. And a prince of a little moment shall bring the other scepter into the other town, and arrows of fire shall be showered from heaven, and many signs and wonders shall be shown.

Then the Antichrist shall rule, and men shall turn aside from the worship of God and become unbelievers, through the coming of him whom they did not seek nor expect, who was an adversary unto all. This man shall be conceived and born of an unholy virgin; and the scepter of imposture shall seize upon the human race during three times and half a time. He will bring the souls of many to perdition, to be partakers of hell forever. Then the angels shall be in anxiety, when they shall see these signs that he showed previously.

And when pious men learn this, they will know and mark the adversary of all mankind, whose signs are these: The joints of his knees are stiff, he is crippled in body, smooth-browed, crooked-fingered long-headed, charming, boastful, intelligent, laughing sweetly, a Seer, discreet, sprightly, meek, quiet, a wonder-worker, having near him the souls of the lost, drawing bread out of stones, making the blind to see the lame to walk, and removing mountains from place to place. All this he will perform in semblance, and many shall believe in him. Woe, to them who shall believe in him and shall take his mark! their eyes shall he closed and turn no more unto Him in Whom they before had hoped.

After this a very great famine shall come. And the heavens shall not shower down rain, and the earth shall not put forth grass; all the fruits shall dry up, and all the inhabitants of the provinces and the towns shall bewail themselves; they shall flee, and they shall not be able to escape, from the east to the west, and from the west to the east; but they that dwell among the mountains, and in the caverns, and in the hollows, and in the clefts of the earth, they only shall be able to flee until the Second coming of Him Who was born of the holy virgin. Then His elect ones shall be known, and they shall see the final coming of the Lord. He shall approach and many shall be judged; there shall be sounds from heaven and much tribulation throughout the world. Woe, to them that are with child and to them that give suck, in the last days! Woe, to the intemperate and to them who shall believe in the Adversary! Woe, to them who worshiped him and declared themselves eager for his coming!

Part XI

The Seventh Vision of Daniel

Chapter Five

And after all this has come to pass, and the Saints and righteous men have suffered torments through poverty and tyranny, then shall the end come. And some amongst men shall point out traces and shall recognize the Seven-Hills, and shall say: 'Has this ever been a city'! And a woman shall go over to the east and to the west, to the north and to the south, and shall find no fruit, but shall find only an olive-tree; and she shall embrace the olive-tree, she shall sigh and say: 'Blessed be he who planted this tree;' and in the same spot her soul shall depart from her.

Then the sun shall be turned into darkness, and the moon into blood, and the stars shall fall down like leaves, and the heavens shall be rolled together as a scroll, and the sea shall bubble up from its depths, and shall overflow to cover all men, and everything shall be burnt and dried by the wind. And the angels of fire shall come down from heaven, and all the universe shall be set on fire. Mice shall appear, flame-shaped and of copper, and like to them, flesh eating savage beasts, shall come out of the mountains and they shall not fear; and he for whom the land of the ungodly sought, shall perish, and the Righteous shall be caught up unto the Father, for a decree has gone out from the Lord. Thrones shall be set up and Books shall be opened, thrones of judgment shall be established, the angels shall sound the trumpet, the Righteous shall rejoice and shall give glory to the Father, and they shall be judged according to their deeds.

But only the Lord is the Righteous Judge. And all his works, and all mankind shall open their mouths, and shall cry and say: 'Lord, Thou Who art the Lord ! lead us not into temptation, but deliver us from evil. For thou, Lord, Who knowest and perceivest that we are not able to bear it, for we are made of flesh, as a beneficent and kindly Father, have pity upon us. For Thine is the glory, now and ever and unto all ages. Amen.'

Part XII

The Fourteenth Vision of Daniel

In the third year of Cyrus the Persian, who captured Babylon, a word was revealed to Daniel, whose name is Balthasar. This word is true. I, Daniel, fasted for twenty-one days until the evening; I had not eaten meat, I had not drunk wine, I had not anointed myself with oil.

It happened, as I was on the bank of the Tigris, that this was revealed to me; I looked; and the four winds of heaven were blowing towards the great sea.

I saw four very frightening animals rising from the river.

The first animal resembled a bear, having wings like an eagle. I saw as I waited that it flew with its wings; a human heart was given to it and it stood on its feet.

The second animal resembled human flesh; excessively horrible, it stood to one side. I watched until three quarters of its face were broken and the fourth quarter remained firm. I looked at it until its teeth were torn out of its mouth.

The third animal resembled a panther; it had wings, four heads, devouring with speed and scattering what remained.

The fourth animal which I saw resembled a lion, an animal much more terrible than all the animals which had been before it. Power and great force were given to it; its hands were of iron, its nails of bronze; devouring, chewing, crushing with its feet what remained. I saw ten horns which came out from its head: I saw also another small horn, which came out beside these ten horns. And great power and a remarkable form were given to it. I saw four different (horns) which arose on its left, then four others which arose after all these; each of them was different from the others, and, between them all, they made nineteen (horns).

And I heard a voice which said to me: "Daniel, do you understand what you saw?" But I said: "How can I understand, if nobody guides me?"

I looked and I saw an angel of God standing on my right. Its wings were extremely bright. I was afraid and I fell to the ground. The angel seized me, made me stand on my feet and said to me:

"Stand on your feet, so that I can proclaim to you what will happen in the last days.

The four animals which you saw are four kingdoms. The animal that you saw, similar to a bear, is the king of Persia. He will possess the land for five hundred fifty-five years. Then he will perish with his kingdom; he will not be powerful for always.

The second animal that you saw, similar to human flesh, it is the king of the Romans: he will seize the land as if by iron; he will extend himself over it; he will dominate by his armies as far as the land of the Ethiopians, and he will reign over it nine hundred and eleven years. But he will not possess the capital of the kingdom, until many days are completed.

The third animal which you saw, who resembled a panther, it is the king of the Greeks. He will reign over it for a thousand years and thirty days; but his reign will not last.

The fourth animal which you saw, who resembles a lion, is the king of the sons of Ishmael. He will reign for a long time over the land and will be very powerful during many days. This realm will be of the race of Abraham and of the slave of Sara, the wife of Abraham. All the cities of the Persians, the Romans and the Greeks will be destroyed; nineteen kings of this race among the sons of Ishmael will reign over the land; they will reign until the time of their end.

The tenth of their kings will be like a prophet, the number of his name is 399. He will practice justice, will give bread to the famished, clothing to those which are naked. He will free those who are slaves. His mercy will spread over the whole land, and his justice up to heaven.

The eleventh of their kings will practice iniquity over all the land; he will ruin the old works. He will persecute those which are on the land, so that nobody is found who lives there or remains there. All men will groan for forty-two months. If the God of heaven treats him with indulgence, his reign will last forty months.

The reign of the twelfth of their kings will consequently be strengthened by the judgements of his mouth. He will carry out malicious actions in the land, so much that men will be astonished by what he did. There will be many wars during his reign. At the end of the time, a king will thoroughly disturb the kingdom of Ismaelites for one hundred and forty-seven years. In the hundred and tenth year of his reign, he will have a war with the Ethiopians. The Ismaelites will reign over them, until they have despoiled the city of the kingdom, which is Souban. They will send messengers to ask for peace; they will give them money and gold in great quantity, a tribute will be paid to them in Ethiopia.

The thirteenth of them will not live in this kingdom at all, and they will not fear him. His reign will be of a few days.

The fourteenth of their kings will receive gold and money in great quantity and he will judge the land with equity. He will engage in war with Lower Egypt, so that Egypt is in sorrow and groaning. The Ethiopians will not be subjected at all to him, they will not pay him tribute. In those days there will be war in the land of the Romans. The Ethiopians will make war with the southernmost regions of Egypt; they will plunder the boroughs and all the cities of lower Egypt, until they arrive at the town of Cleopatra that she built herself in Upper Egypt, which city is Schmoun. After these things, the king of Syria will learn of it, he will fear the end because the war is approaching him. In the end, his reign will be established and he will enjoy a happy existence.

Then a child will arise among the Israelites will rise; this is the fifteenth of their kings. In his heart, he will be hard like iron; he will extend his sword to the Romans; his right hand will be on the Ethiopians. His face will be double and his language will be double. During the days of his reign, there will be a great disorder over all the land, and his word will be violent like fire. The Ethiopians will bring gifts of gold to him, of silver, of pearls, and he will impose his work on everyone. He will make several nations captive in order to conscript them; throughout all his reign, there will not be enough bread; there will be no peace as long as he will reign, and in his time carnage will be frequent.

As for the sixteenth of their kings, there will be no war in his kingdom, and he himself will not fight with anybody, and he will be granted a long time (which he will spend) in peace, and his reign will pass in uprightness.

As regards the seventeenth of their kings, a war will break out between him and his nation; it is him whose name makes the number 666. He will elevate from his nation a man who will make war for him; he will pursue him as far as Egypt with the riches of its kingdom. He will neglect his nation and its great people and will scatter riches in public places and highways. While moving in lower Egypt with his riches, he will go into Upper Egypt on the side of the North, with the intention to plunder Souban, the city of the Ethiopians, with the remainder of its riches. But a man of his own nation will kill him in the southernmost regions of lower Egypt, and will take what remains to him of his riches.

The eighteenth of their kings, at the beginning of his reign, will work great evils, for one thousand, two hundred and sixty days. He will wage war in the western countries, and he will gain the victory until the day of his death.

Then among them a child will arise, who is his son. This one is the nineteenth of their kings. He will be the child of a double race, because his father is an Israelite, his mother is Roman. There will be war in Egypt and Syria for twenty-one months. Their swords will fall on themselves in this war. This is the king whose name makes the number 666; he will be called by these three names: Mametios, Khalle and Sarapidos. Being a child, he will reign in order to do much evil. He will order all the Jews which are in all places to gather in Jerusalem.

All the land will be disturbed during his reign, until any man can be sold for a single dinar. He is without decency and he will forget the fear of God. He will not remember the law of Ishmael his father, nor of his mother, who is Roman; he will be arrogant, continuously drunk; he will make a great number of those who eat at his table die by poisoned beverages, and in these days there will be great devastations. He will free Syria and the territory of Jews, and will torment the East and Egypt. He will establish carriers of letters in Egypt. Two and three times in only one year, the East will be against itself in this reign which will be the nineteeth. He will seek neither justice, nor truth, but he will seek gold all the time. He will establish managers in the regions of Africa, and a great quantity of soldiers. War will break out between him and them; they will destroy the multitude which is with him; he will be established in the regions of Africa, with what will remain of his troops, for several years, and he will not overcome it. Then a foreign nation will rise against him; it is called Pitourgos; it will make war on him. Sarapidos will dominate over many Romans, over Pentapolis, over the Medes; from them all he will take a tribute, will command their cities and will plunder the city which he built, and regions that his father had gathered.

The Turk will prepare for war to remove the kingdom from the hands of Sarapidos; hitherto Sarapidos remained at home. He was looking for spoils, because Sarapidos had great riches before his eyes, gold, silver, all kinds of precious stones, and desirable utensils of every kind. But it will be proclaimed to him that the Turk has made himself Master of all Syria and his borders, and he will go out in great disorder with all his troops; he will leave all the water-skins, will not carry anything with him; but he will have a heart of an animal, reflecting and knowing not what to do. Then, when he flees, going up Egypt, the Turk will precede him with his troops. They will both land with their troops, they will fight until blood runs in floods. The Turk is of Roman race. There will be war at Eschmoun the city, until the water of the river is changed into blood because of the great quantity of those wounded to death. No-one will be able to drink the water any more. Many men will die by the sword, uncountable. Those who remain will plunder their own country from where they left. The Turk will make Sarapidos perish, in order to remove his kingdom from him, for fear he will not obtain the kingdom of the Ishmaelites; but this is here the end of their number.

Then the king of the Romans will rise up against them, he will destroy them by the edge of the sword in the middle of the Ishmaelites in the territory of their fathers in the desert. The Ishmaelites will be governed always by the Romans; the

Romans will dominate over Egypt for forty years.

Then two nations will rise, by the name of Gog and Magog; they will shake the ground for several days; their number is as great as the grains of sand.

Then Antichrist will appear who will deceive many of them. When he is strengthened, he will seduce even the elect. He will kill the two prophets Enoch and Elias, so that for three and a half days they will be dead in the public places of the great town of Jerusalem.

Then the Ancient of Days will bring them back to life. It is He whom I see coming with the clouds from Heaven, similar to a son of man. His power is an eternal power and His reign will have no end. It is he which will put Antichrist to death and all the multitude which is with him. There will be misfortune then in truth to any soul who will live in that time over all the land, because there will be iniquity, a great affliction and groanings; but the salvation of man is between the hands of God in Heaven. This is the end of the speech."

The angel said to me: "Daniel, Daniel, conceal these discourses, seal them up until the time when they will be fulfilled, because that is the end of all." I, Daniel, I arose, I put a seal to the discourse, and sealed them. I will glorify God, the father of all things and the lord of the universe, He who knows the dates and times. To him be glory and power forever. Amen.

www.ingramcontent.com/pod-product-compliance
Lightning Source LLC
LaVergne TN
LVHW041458070426
835507LV00009B/663